My United States

Pennsylvania

KAREN KELLAHER

Children's Press®
An Imprint of Scholastic Inc.

Content Consultant
James Wolfinger, PhD, Associate Dean and Professor
College of Education, DePaul University, Chicago, Illinois

Library of Congress Cataloging-in-Publication Data
Names: Kellaher, Karen, author.
Title: Pennsylvania / by Karen Kellaher.
Description: New York, NY : Children's Press, an imprint of Scholastic Inc., 2018. | Series: A true book | Includes
   bibliographical references and index.
Identifiers: LCCN 2017051376 | ISBN 9780531235768 (library binding) | ISBN 9780531250891 (pbk.).
Subjects: LCSH: Pennsylvania—Juvenile literature.
Classification: LCC F149.3 .K45 2018 | DDC 974.8—dc23
LC record available at https://lccn.loc.gov/2017051376

Front cover: Amish farmers

Back cover: Hot pretzels

Welcome to Pennsylvania

Find the Truth!

Everything you are about to read is true **except** for one of the sentences on this page.

Which one is **TRUE**?

T or F America's first hospital was built in Pennsylvania.

T or F Pennsylvania is mostly flat.

KEYSTONE STATE
BPP·1852
PENNSYLVANIA

Find the answers in this book.

Contents

1 Land and Wildlife

2 Government

THE BIG TRUTH!

What Represents Pennsylvania?

Mountain laurel

Brook trout

Groundhog Day

3 History

4 Culture

Great Dane

This Is Pennsylvania!

CANADA

LAKE ERIE

NEW YORK

ERIE

OHIO

Allegheny

Andy Warhol Museum

Penn State

Allegheny Plateau

Little League Baseball Museum

Susquehanna

Lackawanna Coal Mine

SCRANTON

Punxsutawney Phil

W. Br. Susquehanna

WILLIAMSPORT

WILKES-BARRE

Carnegie Museum of Natural History

Crayola Experience

Susquehanna

Delaware

NEW JERSEY

PENNSYLVANIA

HARRISBURG

ALLENTOWN

1 Pittsburgh's Inclined Railways

PITTSBURGH

2 Hershey

Valley Forge National Historical Park

4

Independe

Monongahela

Allegheny Mountains

Gettysburg National Military Park

3

National Watch & Clock Museum

PHILADELPHIA

U.S. Mint

Franklin Institute

WEST VIRGINIA

MARYLAND

Chesapeake Bay

Delaware Bay

DELAWARE

Washington, D.C.

Independence National Historical Park

ATL
O

N
W E
S

0   40
Miles

VIRGINIA

6

① Pittsburgh's Inclined Railways

The city of Pittsburgh has many steep hills. In the 1800s, special railways were built to move people and goods up and down the slopes. Motorized cables lifted and lowered the cars. Today, two of those railways still operate.

② Hershey

In 1900, Milton S. Hershey built a chocolate factory in southeastern Pennsylvania. Today, Hershey is a bustling city, and Hersheypark is popular for its rides and sweet treats.

NEW YORK

③ Gettysburg National Military Park

This is the site of the Battle of Gettysburg, one of the most important battles in America's Civil War. Nearby is the spot where President Abraham Lincoln gave his famous Gettysburg Address, honoring the soldiers who died in the battle.

④ Independence Hall

On July 4, 1776, America's Founding Fathers approved the Declaration of Independence at this historic building. It is also where they signed the U.S. Constitution on September 17, 1787.

Hay is the number one crop grown in Pennsylvania.

CHAPTER 1

Land and Wildlife

Pennsylvania is located in the mid-Atlantic region of the United States. With an area of just 46,055 square miles (119,282 square kilometers), it is not a huge state. But it is big on natural beauty. Pennsylvania is known for its rolling hills and green valleys. It contains breathtaking rivers, lakes, and waterfalls. More than half of the state is covered in forestland, which provides a perfect **habitat** for many kinds of wildlife.

Hills and Valleys

The northwestern and southeastern corners of Pennsylvania are low and flat. In between these areas, much of the **terrain** is hilly. Pennsylvania's largest land region is the Appalachian Plateau. Its high mountain ridges cover about two-thirds of the state. The state's lowest point is on its eastern border along the Delaware River. Here, the land sits at sea level.

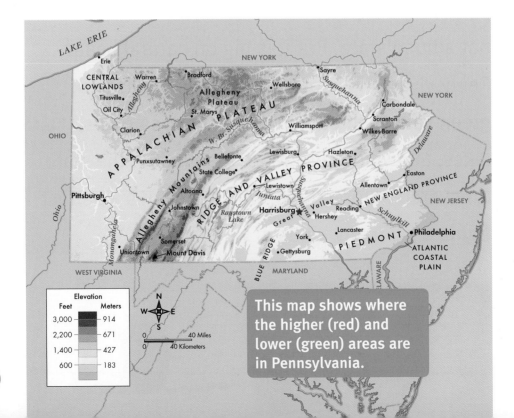

This map shows where the higher (red) and lower (green) areas are in Pennsylvania.

Rock Music

Ringing Rocks Park in southeastern Pennsylvania is one of the state's natural wonders. It is a field of boulders piled about 10 feet (3 meters) high. But these are no ordinary rocks. Many of them ring like bells when they are struck by hammers!

The rock pile formed many thousands of years ago, when water got into cracks in the rocky ground. The water froze, melted, and froze again—over and over. This caused the ground to break into rocky chunks. Scientists are not sure exactly what makes the rocks ring.

Visitors strike rocks with hammers at Ringing Rocks Park. The rocks that create bell-like ringing sounds are often called "live ones."

Pennsylvania Waterways

Pennsylvania has three major river systems. The Delaware River separates Pennsylvania from New Jersey to the east. The Susquehanna River flows through the east-central part of the state. The Allegheny River twists and turns through northwestern Pennsylvania. The state also has dozens of natural lakes and about 2,500 human-made ones. In the northwestern corner, it has about 50 miles (80 km) of shoreline along Lake Erie.

A Varied Climate

Pennsylvanians need to dress for all kinds of weather! Summertime temperatures often top 90 degrees Fahrenheit (32 degrees Celsius). Winter brings a chill, with temperatures frequently dipping below the freezing point. Pennsylvania also gets plenty of rain and snow.

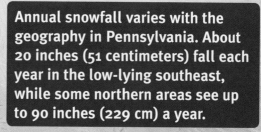

MAXIMUM TEMPERATURE	MINIMUM TEMPERATURE
111 °F	-42 °F

Annual snowfall varies with the geography in Pennsylvania. About 20 inches (51 centimeters) fall each year in the low-lying southeast, while some northern areas see up to 90 inches (229 cm) a year.

The Colors of Nature

More than 100 tree species grow in Pennsylvania's thick woodlands. They include maple, beech, white and yellow pine, hickory, and birch trees.

The state also has thousands of species of shrubs and wildflowers. Be on the lookout for colorful azaleas, rhododendrons, honeysuckles, and mountain laurels, the official state flower.

Allegheny National Forest covers about 517,000 acres (209,222 hectares) in northern Pennsylvania.

Peregrine falcons can dive through the air at speeds of more than 200 miles (322 km) per hour.

Wild Things

Pennsylvania's land, waterways, and skies are home to diverse wildlife. White-tailed deer, black bears, and other mammals fill the state's forests and fields. Fish species such as pickerel, bass, and trout swim in lakes and rivers. Robins, bluebirds, and peregrine falcons fly overhead. Pennsylvania has several animals that are **endangered**. One is the Indiana bat. It is in danger of dying out partly because of an easily spread disease called white-nose syndrome.

Pennsylvania's capital, Harrisburg, is named for John Harris, who donated a parcel of land along the Susquehanna River.

Government

Pennsylvania's capital city is Harrisburg, but that has not always been the case. In Pennsylvania's earliest days, its government was based in Philadelphia. In 1799, the capital moved to Lancaster. In 1812, it moved to its present location. The capitol, the building where state lawmakers meet, was rebuilt twice before the current one was finished in 1906. It is known for its large dome.

Three Branches

Pennsylvania's state government has three branches. The governor is in charge of the executive branch, which enforces the state's laws. The General Assembly is the legislative branch. It has two parts—the Senate and the House of Representatives—and makes the state's laws. The state's courts make up the judicial branch.

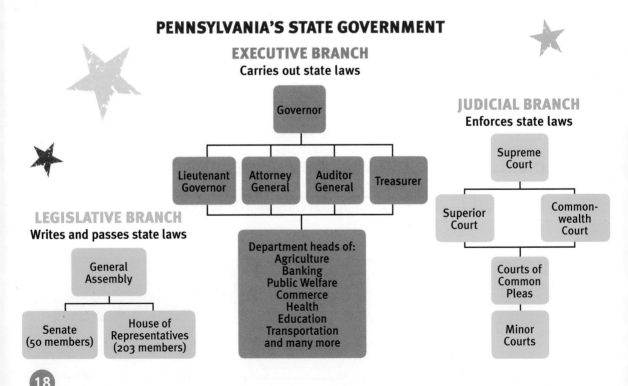

PENNSYLVANIA'S STATE GOVERNMENT

EXECUTIVE BRANCH
Carries out state laws

Governor

Lieutenant Governor | Attorney General | Auditor General | Treasurer

Department heads of:
Agriculture
Banking
Public Welfare
Commerce
Health
Education
Transportation
and many more

JUDICIAL BRANCH
Enforces state laws

Supreme Court

Superior Court | Commonwealth Court

Courts of Common Pleas

Minor Courts

LEGISLATIVE BRANCH
Writes and passes state laws

General Assembly

Senate (50 members) | House of Representatives (203 members)

What's in a Name?

In its state constitution, Pennsylvania calls itself a *commonwealth*. Commonwealth is a different word for "state." In particular, the word is often used to refer to a state or a government that works for the good of its people, rather than the

The people of Pennsylvania are proud of their state's history as a commonwealth.

good of a king or some other leader. Pennsylvania is one of four U.S. states that chose to be called commonwealths when they were formed. The others are Massachusetts, Virginia, and Kentucky.

Pennsylvania's National Role

Each state elects officials to represent it in the U.S. Congress. Like every state, Pennsylvania has two senators. The U.S. House of Representatives relies on a state's population to determine its numbers. Pennsylvania has 18 representatives in the House.

Every four years, states vote on the next U.S. president. Each state is granted a number of electoral votes based on its number of members of Congress. With two senators and 18 representatives, Pennsylvania has 20 electoral votes.

2 senators and 18 representatives

20 electoral votes

With 20 electoral votes, Pennsylvania's voice in presidential elections is above average.

The People of Pennsylvania

Elected officials in Pennsylvania represent a population with a range of interests, lifestyles, and backgrounds.

Ethnicity (2016 estimates)

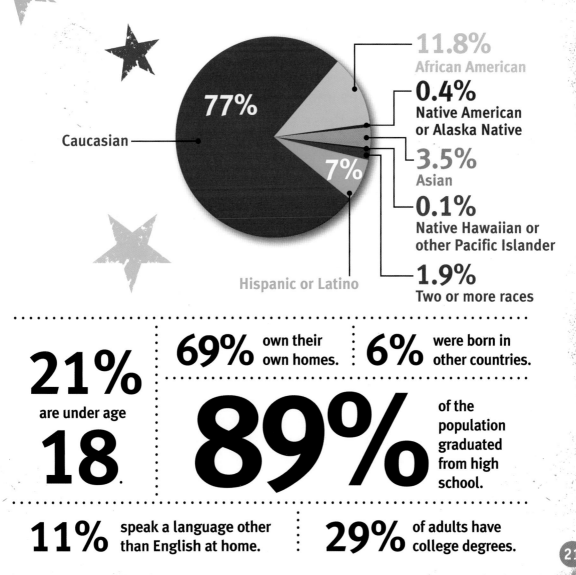

77%
Caucasian

11.8%
African American

0.4%
Native American or Alaska Native

3.5%
Asian

0.1%
Native Hawaiian or other Pacific Islander

1.9%
Two or more races

7%
Hispanic or Latino

21% are under age **18**.

69% own their own homes.

6% were born in other countries.

89% of the population graduated from high school.

11% speak a language other than English at home.

29% of adults have college degrees.

What Represents Pennsylvania?

States choose specific animals, plants, and objects to represent the values and characteristics of the land and its people. Find out why these symbols were chosen to represent Pennsylvania or discover surprising curiosities about them.

Seal

Pennsylvania adopted its seal in 1791. The front of the seal has a ship (representing trade), a plow (representing natural resources), and bundles of wheat (representing agriculture). The bald eagle stands for the United States. The corn on the left represents Pennsylvania's agricultural past. The olive branch on the right symbolizes a peaceful future.

Flag

The state flag, approved in 1799, has many of the same symbols as the seal. It also includes the state motto: Virtue, Liberty, and Independence.

Great Dane

STATE DOG
Pennsylvania's founder, William Penn, brought his Great Danes to America from England.

Brook Trout

STATE FISH
This is the only trout species native to Pennsylvania.

Mountain Laurel

STATE FLOWER
These star-shaped flowers grow on small shrubs that grow wild in Pennsylvania.

White-Tailed Deer

STATE ANIMAL
Pennsylvania has about 30 deer per 1 square mile (2.6 sq km).

Milk

STATE BEVERAGE
Pennsylvania is one of the top 10 milk-producing states.

Ruffed Grouse

STATE BIRD
Found in Pennsylvania's forests, this bird can fly but spends most of its time on the ground or in trees.

The Battle of Gettysburg was the single bloodiest conflict of the Civil War. At least 43,000 people were killed or injured in the fight.

CHAPTER 3

History

The name *Pennsylvania* means "Penn's woods." In the mid-1600s, a man named William Penn was spreading a new religion in England. People who practiced it were called Quakers. But England allowed only one religion, the Church of England. Penn dreamed of creating a place where people could practice any religion. He asked the king of England for land in America, where England had **colonies**. The king owed money to William Penn's father, so he gave Penn land to settle the debt. The colony was named Pennsylvania in honor of Penn's father.

Native Americans

People lived in the area that is now Pennsylvania long before it was an English colony. The first humans arrived there at least 12,000 years ago. They survived by hunting wild animals and collecting berries, fruits, and nuts. Around 3,000 years ago, people in the area began planting crops. Soon they were expert farmers growing fields full of squash, corn, and beans. These crops are sometimes called the Three Sisters because they grow well near each other.

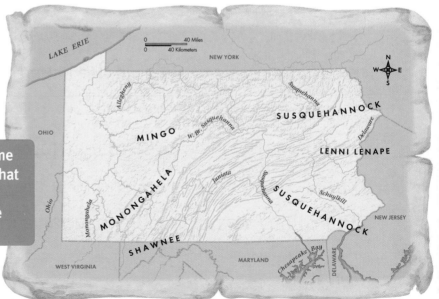

This map shows some of the major tribes that lived in what is now Pennsylvania before Europeans came.

The Susquehannock people lived in small villages along the Susquehanna River.

The area's Native Americans formed many tribes, including the Monongahela, the Susquehannock, and the Lenni Lenape. The Monongahela lived in southwestern Pennsylvania. Other tribes attacked them often, and they disappeared by the early 1600s. It is estimated that about 5,000 Susquehannock people were living in North America in the early 1600s. Later, they were devastated by European diseases and killed in clashes with European settlers.

Colonial Times

People from Sweden, the Netherlands, and England began exploring the area that is now Pennsylvania in the early 1600s. By 1664, England claimed the land as its own. And in 1681, William Penn was given his **charter** to set up the colony of Pennsylvania. In 1682, Penn began building a capital city called Philadelphia near the Delaware River. It soon became the largest city in colonial America.

This map shows early forts, villages, and trading posts established by European explorers as they explored and settled what is now Pennsylvania.

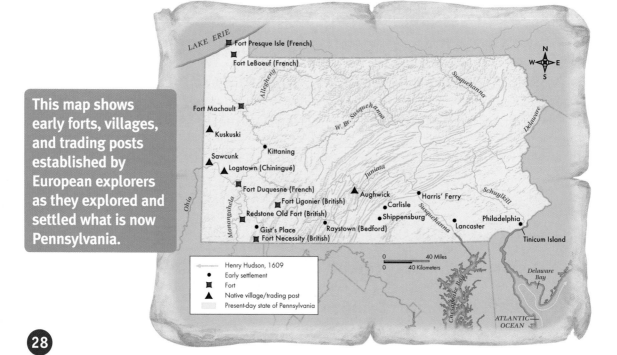

LAKE ERIE
Fort Presque Isle (French)
Fort LeBoeuf (French)
Susquehanna
Allegheny
Delaware
Fort Machault
W. Br. Susquehanna
Kuskuski
Sawcunk • Kittaning
Logstown (Chiningué)
Juniata
Ohio
Monongahela
Fort Duquesne (French)
Fort Ligonier (British)
Redstone Old Fort (British)
Aughwick
Harris' Ferry
Schuylkill
Carlisle
Shippensburg
Susquehanna
Gist's Place
Raystown (Bedford)
Lancaster
Philadelphia
Fort Necessity (British)
Tinicum Island

Henry Hudson, 1609
• Early settlement
⬛ Fort
▲ Native village/trading post
Present-day state of Pennsylvania

0   40 Miles
0   40 Kilometers

Chesapeake Bay
Delaware Bay
ATLANTIC OCEAN

Pennsylvania was the second state to approve the U.S. Constitution, after Delaware.

A Nation Is Born

From 1775 to 1783, the 13 colonies of America fought the Revolutionary War to win independence from Great Britain. Pennsylvania played a key role. In July 1776, colonial leaders met in Philadelphia to sign the Declaration of Independence. Later, many battles took place in Pennsylvania. After the war, the 13 colonies became the United States. In 1787, America's leaders met in Philadelphia to write the U.S. Constitution.

Slavery and Freedom

The issue of **slavery** soon divided the nation. Pennsylvania and other northern states outlawed slavery by the early 1800s, but the practice continued in the South. Disagreements over slavery led to the Civil War (1861–1865). Several battles were fought in Pennsylvania, including the famous Battle of Gettysburg. In 1865, the war ended, and slavery was banned throughout the country.

Timeline of Pennsylvania Events

10,000 BCE
The first people settle in what is now Pennsylvania. Over time, they develop into several unique cultures.

1681
William Penn creates the colony of Pennsylvania.

| 10,000 BCE | 1609 CE | 1681 | 1776 |

1609 CE
The first Europeans explore the area.

1776
The 13 colonies declare their independence from Britain.

Ups and Downs

After the Civil War, Pennsylvania's **economy** grew. Pittsburgh became the nation's top steel producer. **Immigrants** poured into the state to work. Like the rest of the nation, Pennsylvania had a rough time during the 1930s, a period known as the Great Depression. Many residents were out of work. The economy improved during World War II (1939–1945), when Pennsylvania's factories produced supplies.

1863
President Abraham Lincoln delivers the Gettysburg Address in Pennsylvania.

2001
During the September 11 terrorist attacks, Flight 93 crashes into a field in Shanksville, Pennsylvania.

1787 — **1863** — **1910** — **2001**

December 12, 1787
Pennsylvania becomes the second state.

1910
Pittsburgh makes 60 percent of all the steel used in the United States.

No one was killed in the Three Mile Island (pictured) incident, but cleanup took 14 years and cost about 1 billion dollars.

Modern Times

The late 1900s and early 2000s brought new challenges for Pennsylvania. In 1979, an accident at Three Mile Island, a nuclear power plant, made many Americans question the safety of nuclear energy.

On September 11, 2001, tragedy struck. **Terrorists** flew planes into several buildings in the United States. As one plane flew over Pennsylvania, passengers bravely fought the terrorists, and the plane crashed into the ground near Shanksville. Everyone on board died.

Among Benjamin Franklin's many achievements, he was the inventor of bifocal glasses, which many people rely on to improve their vision even today.

Benjamin Franklin: Statesman and Scientist

Peek at a $100 bill, and you'll see the face of one of Pennsylvania's most famous residents. Benjamin Franklin was born in Massachusetts in 1706 and moved to Philadelphia as a teenager. There, he published a newspaper and an **annual** book of facts and clever sayings called *Poor Richard's Almanack*. He also helped build the nation's first hospital and volunteer fire department, both in Philadelphia. Additionally, Franklin was an inventor and scientist. He invented the lightning rod after doing experiments with electricity. But Franklin is best known for his role as a Founding Father. He signed both the Declaration of Independence and the U.S. Constitution.

Andy Warhol's famous painting of rock-and-roll singer Elvis Presley hangs in Pittsburgh's Andy Warhol Museum.

CHAPTER 4

Culture

Pennsylvania has a rich and diverse culture. One important part of that culture is art. The state has more than 30 art museums, including the Philadelphia Museum of Art and Pittsburgh's Carnegie Museum of Art. They feature paintings, sculptures, and other works, including many by native Pennsylvania artists. For example, one museum in Pittsburgh highlights the art of Andy Warhol. He was known for painting famous people and everyday objects like soup cans.

Sports and Recreation

Pennsylvania's mountains, rivers, and parks are perfect for outdoor activities like biking, boating, fishing, and hiking. When winter rolls around, skiers hit the slopes at more than 20 resorts.

Many professional sports teams call Pennsylvania home.

Robert Covington of the Philadelphia 76ers dunks the ball during a 2018 home game at Philadelphia's Wells Fargo Center.

The Steelers, Penguins, and Pirates all play in Pittsburgh. The Eagles, Phillies, Flyers, and 76ers play in Philadelphia.

Time to Celebrate!

In Pennsylvania, the year starts with the Mummers Parade, held in Philadelphia every New Year's Day. The mummers are performers who dress in fancy costumes, dance, and play instruments. In February, the town of Punxsutawney hosts the nation's biggest Groundhog Day celebration. In the summer, Pennsylvanians flock to local and county fairs to enjoy rides, games, and treats.

During Punxsutawney's Groundhog Day celebration, tens of thousands of people gather each year to find out whether a groundhog named Punxsutawney Phil will predict six more weeks of winter weather.

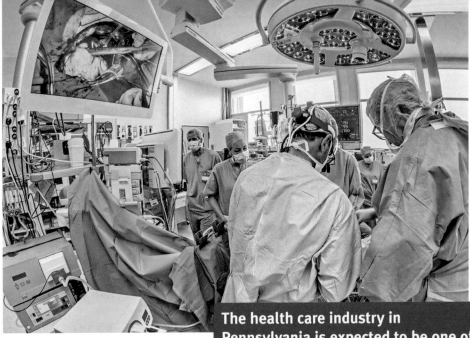

The health care industry in Pennsylvania is expected to be one of the fastest-growing sources of jobs in the state over the next few years.

On the Job

Pennsylvanians have many types of jobs. Tens of thousands of people in the state make a living by farming or mining coal, limestone, or gravel. More than 500,000 people work in **manufacturing**. They produce everything from chemicals and computers to medicines and snack foods. And millions of Pennsylvanians have jobs in service-related fields such as education, healthcare, banking, food service, and tourism.

A Simple Life

In southeastern Pennsylvania's Lancaster County, it's common to see horse-drawn buggies on the roads. This area is home to a religious group known as the Amish. Amish people lead simple lives in small farming communities. They do not drive cars or use modern electric appliances.

The Amish wear simple, plain clothing. Women wear long dresses, while men wear either suits or sturdy work clothes. Among themselves, most Amish people speak a version of German called Pennsylvania Dutch.

What's to Eat?

No visitor leaves Pennsylvania hungry! Dumplings called pierogies are popular in Pittsburgh. Philadelphia is known for its cheesesteaks. These sandwiches are made with thin slices of beef and melted cheese. Another favorite food in the state is shoofly pie, a sweet Pennsylvania Dutch treat.

Soft Pretzels

Ask an adult to help you!

Pennsylvania produces 80 percent of America's pretzels! These salty snacks were brought to Pennsylvania by German immigrants in the 1700s.

Ingredients

1 package dry yeast
1 $1/_2$ cups warm water
1 tablespoon sugar
1 teaspoon salt
4 cups bread flour

1 egg
1 tablespoon water
Extra salt for topping
  (kosher salt works well)

Directions

Preheat the oven to 425 degrees. Dissolve the yeast in the water. Add the sugar and salt, and stir. Slowly stir in 3 $1/_2$ cups of the flour. If the dough feels sticky, add up to another $1/_2$ cup flour. Knead the dough with your hands for 10 minutes. Divide it into 14 portions, and roll each portion into a rope. Bend the ropes into pretzel shapes. Place the pretzels on a baking sheet lined with parchment paper. Beat the egg and 1 tablespoon water together. Brush this mixture onto the tops of the pretzels. Sprinkle with salt, then bake for 15 minutes.

Valley Forge National Historical Park, located in southeastern Pennsylvania, marks the location where American forces spent the winter of 1777–1778 during the American Revolution.

Something for Everyone

Pennsylvania is one of America's oldest states—and also one of the most interesting. With its natural beauty, diverse population, and rich culture and history, it has a lot to offer. Some of the Keystone State's major features include mountain trails, lush forests, historic battlefields and buildings, folk festivals, theme parks, and bustling cities. Each year, millions of tourists visit the state to take it all in. More than 12 million Pennsylvania residents get to enjoy these attractions all year long. ★

Famous People

James Buchanan

(1791–1868) served as America's 15th president and is the country's only president from Pennsylvania. He led the nation in the years leading to the Civil War.

Milton Hershey

(1857–1945) started the Hershey Chocolate Company and built the town of Hershey. His treats were less expensive than other chocolates. That meant more people could enjoy them.

Louisa May Alcott

(1832–1888) was a famous author. Her most successful book was *Little Women*, about four sisters growing up in the 1800s. She was from Germantown, a neighborhood in Philadelphia.

Elizabeth Cochran

(1864–1922) was a newspaper reporter better known by her pen name, Nellie Bly. She wrote about serious topics, such as conditions in U.S. factories. In 1889, she made a trip around the world in 72 days and wrote about it. She was a native of the Pittsburgh area.

Marian Anderson

(1897–1993) was the first African American singer to perform with the New York Metropolitan Opera. She was born in Philadelphia.

Rachel Carson

(1907–1964) was a scientist and environmentalist whose 1962 book *Silent Spring* helped people understand the dangers of pollution. She was from Springdale.

Andrew Wyeth

(1917–2009) was a popular artist who often painted scenes from the Pennsylvania countryside. His father, N. C. Wyeth, was also a famous artist.

Bayard Rustin

(1912–1987) was an activist who fought for the rights of African Americans during the civil rights movement. He was from West Chester.

Wilt Chamberlain

(1936–1999) played for the Philadelphia Warriors and several other National Basketball Association teams during a long career. In 1962, he set a league record by scoring 100 points for the Warriors in a single game. He was born in Philadelphia.

Taylor Swift

(1989–) is an award-winning singer-songwriter who has sold millions of albums. She is from Reading.

Guion Bluford

(1942–) is a former astronaut for the National Aeronautics and Space Administration. In 1983, he became the first African American to travel in space. He was born and raised in Philadelphia.

Did You Know That . . .

Pennsylvania's nickname is the Keystone State. A keystone is the middle stone in an archway. It helps hold the arch together. Back in colonial times, Pennsylvania was the middle colony.

Pittsburgh has 446 bridges—more than any other city in the world! They help people cross the city's many creeks and rivers. As a result, Pittsburgh's nickname is the City of Bridges.

The first U.S. Mint opened in Philadelphia in 1792. Its job was to make coins for the nation. Today, the U.S. Mint facility there makes more than 8 billion coins per year.

The small town of Kennett Square is known as the mushroom capital of the world. Farmers in and around the town grow about one million mushrooms every week. How do they do it? One secret is spreading lots of horse manure on the soil.

The historic Liberty Bell is a symbol of American freedom. It arrived in Philadelphia in 1752 and was famously rung in July 1776, when the Founding Fathers read the Declaration of Independence to the public. Sometime in the 1800s, it developed a large crack, affecting its sound.

A Pittsburgh scientist named Jonas Salk developed the first vaccine to prevent polio in 1952. Polio was a disease that killed thousands of Americans and left many others paralyzed every year in the early 1900s. After Salk created his vaccine, the disease became very rare.

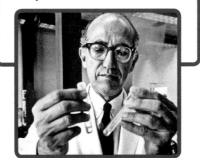

The Crayola crayon company produces 12 million crayons a day in its Easton, Pennsylvania, factory. It currently makes crayons in 120 standard colors.

Did you find the truth?

T America's first hospital was built in Pennsylvania.

F Pennsylvania is mostly flat.

Resources

Books

Cunningham, Kevin. *The Pennsylvania Colony.* New York: Children's Press, 2012.

Gregory, Josh. *The Revolutionary War.* New York: Children's Press, 2010.

Hasan, Heather. *Pennsylvania: Past and Present.* New York: Rosen, 2010.

Jerome, Kate Boehm. *Pennsylvania: What's So Great About This State?* Charleston, SC: Arcadia Kids, 2011.

Maine, Tyler. *Pennsylvania.* Mankato, MN: Capstone Press, 2016.

Rozett, Louise (ed.). *Fast Facts About the 50 States: Plus Puerto Rico and Washington, D.C.* New York: Children's Press, 2010.

Visit this Scholastic website for more information on Pennsylvania:
★ www.factsfornow.scholastic.com
Enter the keyword **Pennsylvania**

Important Words

annual (AN-yoo-uhl) happening once every year

charter (CHAHR-tur) a formal document that states the rights or duties of a group of people

colonies (KAH-luh-neez) territories that have been settled by people from another country and are controlled by that country

economy (ih-KAH-nuh-mee) the system of buying, selling, making things, and managing money in a place

endangered (en-DAYN-jurd) in danger of becoming extinct, usually due to human activity

habitat (HAB-i-tat) the place and natural conditions in which a plant or animal lives

immigrants (IM-i-gruhnts) people who come from abroad to live permanently in a country

manufacturing (man-yuh-FAK-chur-ing) making something, often with machines

slavery (SLAY-vur-ee) the practice of keeping other people as property and forcing them to work without pay

terrain (tuh-RAYN) an area of land

terrorists (TER-ur-ists) people who use violence and fear to achieve their goals

Index

Page numbers in **bold** indicate illustrations.

About the Author

Karen Kellaher is an editor in Scholastic's classroom magazine division and has written more than 20 books for kids and teachers. A New Jersey resident originally from the Philadelphia area, she still roots for the "Iggles" and enjoys a good cheesesteak. Kellaher holds a bachelor's degree in communications from the University of Scranton and a master's degree combining elementary education and publishing from New York University's Gallatin School of Individualized Study.